One Eternal Round

COLORING BOOK

by AMBER DAWN KYLE

CFI • An Imprint of Cedar Fort, Inc.
Springville, Utah

Dedicated to my missionary son, Elder Jameson, and to all missionaries, who want to serve with all their heart, might, mind and strength.

—Amber

ISBN 13: 978-1-4621-4990-2

Published by CFI, an imprint of Cedar Fort, Inc.
2373 W. 700 S., Suite 100, Springville, UT 84663
Distributed by Cedar Fort, Inc., www.cedarfort.com

Cover design and interior layout by Shawnda T. Craig
Cover design © 2025 Cedar Fort, Inc.
Edited by Kyle Lund

Printed in the United States of America

10 9 8 7 6 5 4 3 2 1

Printed on acid-free paper

This book belongs to

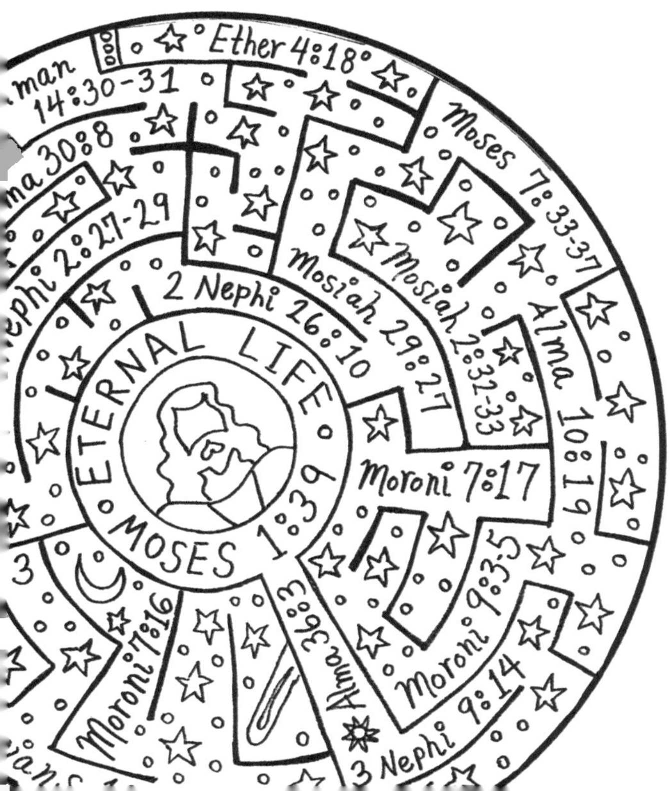

ONE ETERNAL ROUND

...THE COURSE OF THE LORD IS ONE ETERNAL ROUND.

—1 NEPHI 10:19

Wherefore, whoso believeth in God might with surety hope for a better world . . . which hope cometh of faith . . .

—Ether 12:4

God's Love Is There

"God's love is there for you whether or not you feel you deserve love. It is simply always there."

—Thomas S. Monson, "We Never Walk Alone", Oct. 2013

God calls prophets by revelation

PROPHETS

Surely the Lord God will do nothing but he revealeth
his secret unto his servants the prophets.

–Amos 3:7

"I saw a pillar of light exactly over my head above the brightness of the sun..."

–Joseph Smith History 1

…if ye have faith ye hope for things which are not seen, which are true.

—Alma 32:21

the Book of Mormon

The Book of Mormon is a volume of holy scripture comparable to the Bible.

–Introduction to The Book of Mormon

LEHI'S DREAM

I beheld a tree, whose fruit
was desirable to make one happy.

—1 Nephi 8

"GOD CARES ABOUT YOU. HE WILL LISTEN.
HE WILL ANSWER YOUR PERSONAL QUESTIONS."

–Elder Dieter F. Uchtdorf, "Receiving a Testimony of Light and Truth",
Oct. 2014 Saturday Morning Session of General Conference.

The Divine Mission of Jesus Christ

"He died, was buried, and rose again the third day, and ascended into heaven…"

—Joseph Smith, Teachings of the Prophet Joseph Smith, 121

I have a family here on earth. They are so good to me. Families can be Together Forever . . .

—HYMN 300

the PLAN of SALVATION

"YOU ARE AND HAVE ALWAYS BEEN A SON OR DAUGHTER OF GOD WITH SPIRITUAL ROOTS IN ETERNITY."

—M. RUSSELL BALLARD, "CHILDREN OF HEAVENLY FATHER", BYU SPEECHES, MARCH 3, 2020.

The Creation

Believe in God . . . that he created all things,
both in heaven and in earth. —Mosiah 4:9

the fall of Adam & Eve

the FALL of ADAM & EVE

Adam fell that men might be; and men are that they might have joy. —2 Nephi 2:25

Have ye experienced this
mighty change in your hearts?

—Alma 5:14

For it is expedient that there should be a great and last sacrifice…
an infinite and eternal sacrifice. —Alma 34: 10

he is
not here
he is
risen

Matthew 28:6

the RESURRECTION of JESUS CHRIST

The Spirit and the body shall be reunited again in its perfect form. —Alma 11:43

Eternal Life

For behold, this is my work and my glory—to bring to pass the immortality and eternal life of man.

—Moses 1:39

the GOSPEL of JESUS CHRIST

For the gate by which ye should enter is repentance and
baptism of water; and then cometh a remission of your
sins by fire and by the Holy Ghost. —2 Nephi 31:17

CHARITY

Charity is the pure love of Christ,
and it endureth forever . . .

—Moroni 7:47

BAPTISM

FOLLOW THOU ME . . . AND BE BAPTIZED
IN THE NAME OF MY BELOVED SON.

–2 NEPHI 31:10–11

the Holy Ghost

"Baptism by water is but half a baptism, and is good for nothing without the other half-that is, the baptism of the Holy Ghost." —Joseph Smith

ENDURE TO THE END

He that endureth to the end, the same shall be saved. —2 Nephi 31:15

THE GREAT COMMANDMENTS

Thou shalt love the Lord thy God with all thy heart, and with all the soul, and with all thy mind...And the second is like unto it, Thou shalt love thy neighbor as thyself. —Matthew 22:37-39

THE TEN COMMANDMENTS

Keep the Commandments—In this there is safety; In this there is peace.

—Hymn 303, Keep the Commandments

the WORD of WISDOM

Given for a principle with promise, adapted to the capacity of the weak and the weakest of all saints . . .
—Doctrine and Covenants 89

the LAW of CHASTITY

Virtue "is a pattern of thought [or] behavior based on high moral standards."
—Preach My Gospel

"Happiness is the object and design of our existence; and will be the end thereof, if we pursue the path that leads to it; the path is virtue." —Joseph Smith

The LAW of the SABBATH

Remember the sabbath day, to keep it holy. —*Exodus 20:8*

the Priesthood

We believe that a man must be called of God, by prophecy, and by the laying on of hands by those who are in authority, to preach the Gospel and administer in the ordinances thereof.

–Article of Faith 5

CHURCH ORGANIZATION

"First and foremost, all the time, we are witnesses of the living reality of the Lord Jesus Christ. We are not administrators; we are ministers of the gospel of Jesus Christ."

—Elder David A. Bednar

the Armor of God

Put on the whole armour of God, that ye may be able to stand against the wiles of the devil.

–Ephesians 6:10–18

For unto us a child is born, unto us a son is given: and the government shall be upon his shoulder: and his name shall be called Wonderful, Counsellor, The mighty God, The everlasting Father, The Prince of Peace. —Isaiah 9:6

Fear not ye; for I know that ye seek Jesus, which was crucified. He is not ere; for he is risen, as he said. Come, see the place where the Lord lay.

—Matthew 28: 5–6

the Eternal Maze

Start at the top and work your way through the maze. Look up each scripture to see which way to choose. Eternal Life or Eternal Death? YOU CHOOSE!

About the Author

Amber Kyle was raised in the south, even though she was born a BYU baby. She claims Northeast Georgia as her home. Amber grew up doodling all throughout her childhood, into high school, and beyond. Instead of listening to her teachers, she would doodle all over her notes, she now teaches piano lessons.

Amber grew up with a father who was the biggest missionary in town, and through his example, learned many ways to do missionary work. She attended Brigham Young University in Provo, and as she worked at the Missionary Training Center as a dishwasher, singing the many hymn's missionaries requested of the dish room, she decided to go on a mission herself. She was called to the Ukraine, Kiev mission where she met many wonderful people.

She now has a husband and one son, who has recently returned from a mission in Colorado. She loves missionary work, and has even helped bring her husband into the gospel due to her missionary efforts. She loves the gospel and the joy it brings as she shares the gospel with everyone around her!